Nature and Child's Life Experiences

Rhodesia

Ukiyoto Publishing

All global publishing rights are held by

Ukiyoto Publishing

Published in 2024

Content Copyright © Rhodesia

ISBN 9789361727467

All rights reserved.
No part of this publication may be reproduced, transmitted, or stored in a retrieval system, in any form by any means, electronic, mechanical, photocopying, recording or otherwise, without the prior permission of the publisher.

The moral rights of the author have been asserted.

This is a work of fiction. Names, characters, businesses, places, events, locales, and incidents are either the products of the author's imagination or used in a fictitious manner. Any resemblance to actual persons, living or dead, or actual events is purely coincidental.

This book is sold subject to the condition that it shall not by way of trade or otherwise, be lent, resold, hired out or otherwise circulated, without the publisher's prior consent, in any form of binding or cover other than that in which it is published.

www.ukiyoto.com

Dedication

For my loving parents Engr. Rodolfo Minguito and Mrs. Evelyn Minguito.

To all the children of the world, this book is for you.

ACKNOWLEDGMENTS

I express my sincerest gratitude to all those who helped me fulfill this book which has been a long-cherished dream in my life:

To our good Lord for blessing me this gift of writing poetry, which I promise to hone and use to inspire others.

To my loving and ever supportive parents, Engr. Rodolfo Minguito and Mrs. Evelyn Minguito who helped me nurture my dreams and achieve my goals in life. Their sound advice enlightened my path and led me in the right direction.

To my understanding, kind and dedicated teachers and administrators at Rosauro Almario Elementary School where I spent primary education, and M. Hizon Elementary School where I continued intermediate education in accelerated class.

To Ukiyoto Publishing, for giving me the platform to share this book to children in other parts of the world.

Contents

Introduction	1
Poems	2
A Beautiful Day	3
Rain	4
Sun	5
Stars	6
Rainbow	7
The Sea	8
Moon	9
Clouds	10
Mountain	11
Sunbeam	12
Water	13
Our Body	14
My Favorite Toy	15
My Pet	16
My Favorite Book	17
God Loves Us	18
My Best Friend	19
Our Family	20
My Mother	21
Dearest Papa	22
Helping At Home	23

My Happiest Birthday	24
My Birthday Wish	25
My Piggy Bank	26
Our School	27
School Days	28
My Teacher	29
United Nations	30
Peace	31
Playtime	32
A Day In The Park	33
At The Mall	34
A Day In The Farm	35
A Day At The Zoo	36
My First Coin	37
My Prayer	38
When I Grow Up	39
My Unlucky Experience	40
My Favorite Flower	41
My Favorite Fruit	42
My Favorite Show	43
A Day At The Beach	44
My Little Plants	45
Let's Plant Trees	46
Pollution Go Away	47
Balloons	48
My Blessed Experience	49

I Wish I Were	50
Graduation Day	51
About the Author	52

Introduction

This book is a compilation of poems of the young Rhodesia from the tender age of five to nine years old, as advised by her teachers and school administrators to compile into a book.

In this book, Rhodesia's poems show the experiences, feelings, desires, dreams, and wishes of a child, as narrated from her unique perspective and language. It also explores a child's questions and curiosity about commonplace themes and objects seen in nature. More than that, her poems are expressions of funny and exciting experiences of her love and concern for others, most especially her parents.

Nature and Child's Life Experiences is a child's desire to share her thoughts, emotions, and goals to all her readers.

2   Nature and Child's Life Experiences

Poems

Poems are written to express beauty,
They inspire people and make them happy,
Even if one doesn't have much money,
Creating things makes one feel wealthy.

It's easy to create and write beautiful poems,
When your mind is rich with imagination,
Especially when you have much inspiration,
It will bring you joy in self expression.

A Beautiful Day

While I was walking down the stairway,
Somebody slid and fell down the stairs,
I was so afraid she might fall away,
So I helped her and held on to her hair.

She embraced me and said "Thank you,
You are very kind, may God bless you!"
I also smiled and said, "Lets be gay,
Because today is a beautiful day!"

Rain

I always wait for the rain to come,
So my plants will grow healthy everytime,
If you want to know the secret of my garden,
It's the love and care that comes from the rain.

I also notice that when it rains,
Some kids like playing and roaming around,
Showering on raindrops is really fun,
That's why I always wait for the rain to come.

Sun

I wonder how the sun gets its bright light.
Why does it not shine during the night?
Did God make the sun to make the world bright,
And to keep us warm so we may stay alive?

Stars

Stars, stars, stars,
I love to see you at night,
You are very far and very bright,
You're like a diamond in my sight.

Twinkling, brightly shining,
Little stars I am wondering,
That someday I'd be walking,
And touching you in my dream.

Rainbow

Look at the rainbow that I love to see,
With its curved colors above and below,
A signal of hope and nature's beauty,
That smiles even after a mighty storm.

The Sea

I love to watch the deep, blue sea,
So big and wide, the end I can't see,
From the big, big sea comes the fish we eat,
When my mother cooks, I really enjoy it!

We have so much fun in the sea,
Swimming, fishing, boating are free,
If you want to relax and be happy,
Then go to the sea with friends and family.

Moon

I wonder how God made the moon
It shines at night, but not at noon,
I wish someday I can go to the moon
They say it's cold, are there no typhoons?

I enjoy playing outdoors when you shine at night,
Or sit at my table cause I'm inspired to write,
Wherever you go, you're always in my sight,
You change your shape from night to night.

Clouds

Clouds, you look like cotton in the sky,
How can I touch you if you're so high?
When your color is gray, it seems you're shy,
And when it is white, you're a lovely sight.

I dream to be with you this day,
Feeling light, carefree, and gay,
Dancing and singing all the way,
Up above, with you, I will stay.

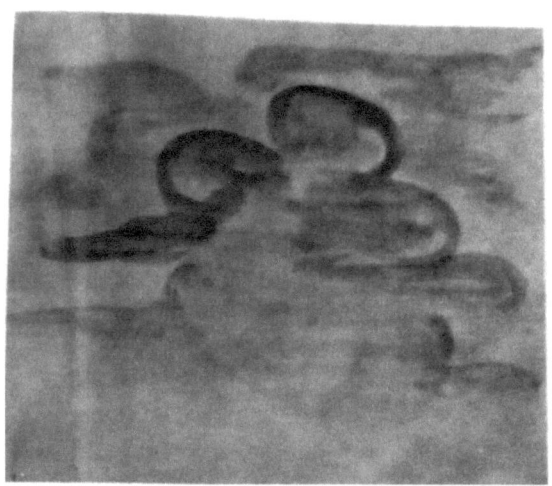

Mountain

I wonder how God created the mountain,
Why does it look like a giant near heaven?
When clouds seem to touch their head,
It's like they are thinking ahead.

l always think how rocks form in this place?
How is the land that wears away replaced?
Can I go up the peak mountain surface,
So that I can feel the air on my face?

Nature and Child's Life Experiences

Sunbeam

When I hear the church bells ringing,
While the roosters are also crowing,
I merrily awake and keep moving,
And open the window where the sun is shining.

Water

I often wonder where water comes from,
Why is it found here and everywhere?
And why do we die without water?
It's really nature's gift to all.

Water is the place where fishes live,
It is also a source of electricity,
We should therefore use water properly,
To avoid shortage in our country.

Our Body

Our body parts have different functions,
Just like a machine when it goes into motion,
Eyes, ears, nose, tongue, and skin for sensation,
Mouth and stomach for digestion.

Joints and muscles permit movement,
Brain and nerves process everything,
Heart, lungs, and blood bring air and nutrients,
Working together to keep us living.

Rhodesia

My Favorite Toy

I have so many pretty toys at home,
Dolls, teddy bear, piano and telephone,
But my favorite is my walking doll,
Because my father brought it home from afar.

I always enjoy playing with my doll,
It is my favorite and best pal,
I sing, dance and care for it,
Always by my side when I sleep.

My Pet

My dog is the best pet I've ever known,
It guards our house and all things we own,
It needs no payment just give it a bone,
It makes me happy and secures our home.

In the afternoon when I'm back home from school,
It does cute tricks that gives me much pleasure,
All the tiredness I feel seem nothing at all,
That's why I love my dog for his awesome behavior.

My Favorite Book

Do you also have a favorite book to read?
Mine has exciting stories illustrated,
While moral lessons are being learned,
So I read my favorite book again and again.

18 Nature and Child's Life Experiences

God Loves Us

I wonder why God created this world,
Why he protects us and gives our daily food,
I'm sure He created everything for us,
Because he loves us, He loves us very much!

My Best Friend

Do you want to know who is my best friend?
She's so good, kind, and loving to children,
She makes our home happy, clean, and in order,
Oh, she's my loving mother!

Whenever I'm sick, she's always at my side,
Giving me her love, proper care and guidance,
If I have any worry, to her I confide,
She supports my dreams and ambitions.

Our Family

We're just a few in the family,
But we are all very happy,
Because we all love one another,
From father down to baby brother.

Earning money is done by father,
Care and protection is given by mother,
Doing the household chores is my sister's share,
And I give them all my love and care.

My Mother

My mother is not just pretty,
She also has an inner beauty,
That's why she's number one to me,
I'll always love her dearly.

Dearest Papa

From morning till night,
I always think of you,
Either the sun is shining bright,
Or the rain is pouring too.

Papa, I'll always love you,
When you're far away, I'm blue,
I can't forget you till I die,
No matter how many days pass by.

Helping At Home

In our small family,
We are all very busy,
Helping one another
Do household chores together.

Father trims the lawn,
Mother does the cooking,
We children clean our home,
So happy that we're helping.

My Happiest Birthday

My last birthday
Was also our school's Recognition Day,
I was very happy my father came home,
He was the one who pinned my ribbon on.

From overseas, he came to see me,
Though I knew he's always very busy,
That was my happiest birthday,
Because Papa was with us, not far away.

Rhodesia

My Birthday Wish

I do not wish for toys,
Like other girls or boys,
I just wish for happiness,
My family, be blessed.

My special birthday wish is this,
Dear God, please cure my mother's heart disease,
Please make her feel better and healthier,
This will make my birthday happier.

My Piggy Bank

Whenever I have money,
Given by my mommy,
Instead of buying candy,
I drop in my small piggy.

Saving a peso each day,
Makes my piggy fatter and gay,
I also learn to be thrifty,
And spend my money wisely.

Our School

Our school is big and wide,
With beautiful rooms inside
It also has a playground,
Where children love to play around.

When there's a visitor in any classroom,
Everyone will stand saying, "Good afternoon!"
Surroundings are clean, with flowers so beautiful,
That is why I love going to our school.

School Days

How happy I am when school day comes near,
New lessons to learn, from teachers so dear,
New friends I meet with smiling faces,
Learning with them brings me happiness.

Beautiful rooms, cool and comfortable
Make learning really so enjoyable,
Reading, writing, singing, and playing,
School days are fun and very exciting.

My Teacher

I have a favorite teacher,
She's kind, understanding, and a very good leader,
She teaches us with love and care,
That's why I really like and love her.

When she is talking and teaching,
All of us are listening,
Cause she tells us amazing things,
That keeps us thinking and also learning.

United Nations

What is the United Nations?
It's a worldwide organization,
That promotes peace and order,
As all nations help one another.

Let's be friends one and all,
Free countries big and small,
All of us are brothers and sisters,
Under one roof of our Mother Earth.

Peace

Peace, peace, peace!
All people like this,
I always pray that peace be in our country,
Open our hearts and minds to have unity.

Playtime

Play time is the best time for me,
Cause I can be happy and carefree,
Playing makes my body healthy,
It also gives me a lot of energy.

Oh, I love to play and play,
After school closes each day,
Playing with my sister and brother,
Gives me lots of fun and laughter.

A Day In The Park

Our family loves to go to the park,
When we are there, we're happy as a lark,
With fresh air, green grass and beautiful flowers,
And playful children, enjoying here and there.

I love watching the colored fountain,
The goldfish in the hidden garden,
But I like best of all a hero's monument,
A day in the park is an unforgettable moment.

At The Mall

We went to a mall with my family,
I rode up the escalator gayly,
But I slid and fell down so suddenly,
Luckily, a kind old man helped and saved me.

A Day In The Farm

One summer day we went to the farm,
We were so happy though the day was warm,
My friends and I had so much fun
Picking fruits under the summer sun.

A Day At The Zoo

One Saturday, we went to the zoo,
I was so happy and excited too,
All kinds of animals were all around,
Big and small, with different sounds.

The birds on the branches,
The monkeys in their cages,
But most attractive of all,
Was the proud peacock so tall!

My First Coin

I was excited with my first coin,
Should I keep it, or buy me a toy?
As I was thinking to save it for morn,
I couldn't find it anymore!

My Prayer

When I was praying,
I asked to win,
In the contest I joined in,
That's creative writing -

"Dear Lord, please make my dream come true,
To make my teachers and parents proud too,
So that I can bring honor to our school
And also reach my dream goal."

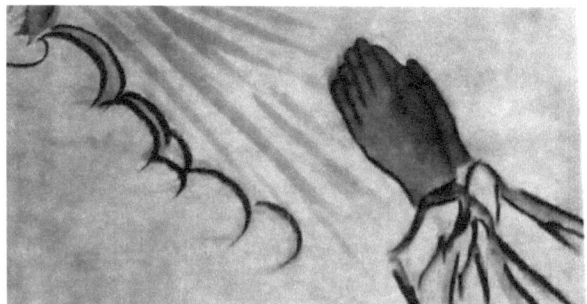

When I Grow Up

When I grow up I will be a doctor,
To my country, I'll give much honor,
I will help sick people become healthy,
Because healthy people are strong and happy.

My Unlucky Experience

We were going to school that day,
"Take care of yourselves," I heard my mother say,
"Cross the street in the proper way,
And before leaving the house, you should pray."

When we were already on the street,
A big truck appeared and I was about to be hit.
My sister pulled my clothes as fast as she could.
That's why I was safe, I never felt so good!

My Favorite Flower

Sampaguita, your buds are small but fragrant,
From afar, the wind carries your sweet scent,
In your petals pure and white,
My heart's at peace, a lovely sight!

My Favorite Fruit

My favorite fruit is the mango,
It is heart-shaped, do you know?
It's not only sweet and delicious,
It is also very nutritious.

My Favorite Show

Once I had a favorite show,
It told stories that happened long ago,
Even took me to places I could not go,
And taught me knowledge I ought to know.

I always wait and watch the show,
Experiencing the high and low,
Like I was really in there also,
It left a lesson before they bow.

A Day At The Beach

One Sunday morning we went to the beach.
With lots of fruits, drinks and biscuits,
We were enjoying swimming in the water,
When all at once a shout came from my sister.

My father swam very fast to save her
Cause my sister had drunk so much water,
I was so happy when she got better,
This day at the beach, I'll always remember!

My Little Plants

I threw some seeds out of the window,
On the seeds fell and shone the rain and the sun,
Soon little leaves began to grow,
I was so excited that my seeds became plants!

Let's Plant Trees

Trees, trees, trees, let's plant trees,
They give us gentle breeze,
Trees gift us clean air to breathe,
And nutritious fruits our bodies need.

Trees give shade and beauty to our country,
They control flood and keep our safety,
Their cool color provides a feeling of peace,
So let's help plant and protect our trees.

Pollution Go Away

Pollution, pollution, go away,
You bring sadness to our day,
Mother cries for her sick child,
When water and air are spoiled.

All of us should do our share,
Avoid throwing trash on bodies of water,
If we plant trees, there'll be fresh air,
And we can enjoy life better.

Balloons

Balloons, balloons, balloons, you're all so pretty!
You give me happiness when you're around me.
What is inside you that makes you fly high?
Please take me with you, when you fly to the sky.

My Blessed Experience

I was seven years of age,
When I entered the creative writing challenge,
My heartbeat was so fast because of nervousness
As this was my first time to join in this contest.

"My Teacher" was the topic given,
So I wrote a poem at that very moment,
When they announced that my poem was the best,
I thanked our Lord for making me so blessed.

I Wish I Were

I wish I were a beautiful flower,
That gives fragrance and sweet smell,
It turns a garden bright and beautiful,
Makes people cheerful, the world wonderful.

A flower that attracts bees and butterflies,
Whose beauty is so pleasing to the eyes,
A flower that makes lonely people smile,
Giving happiness all the while.

Graduation Day

When I think of our graduation day,
I feel its importance, mixed with excitement,
For it is the dream of every student,
To triumphantly march in that event.

Sincerest thanks to our teachers and parents,
For giving us endless support and guidance.
We too promise you, our dearest Alma Mater,
That someday, we will bring you pride and honor.

About the Author

Rhodesia

The young Rhodesia who wrote this book was a nine-year-old grade 6 pupil in accelerated class, and was then the lone public school pupil ever known to have put out a collection of literary pieces in book form. She had consistently won honors for her school in creative writing and academic competitions.

Rhodesia's shining accomplishments had not spoiled her unassuming ways. She was aptly described by her parents as deeply religious, obedient, and loving. In fact she was actively engaged in activities for the out-of-school youths in her local community.

www.ingramcontent.com/pod-product-compliance
Lightning Source LLC
LaVergne TN
LVHW041549070526
838199LV00046B/1883